Meet Cam the Cow

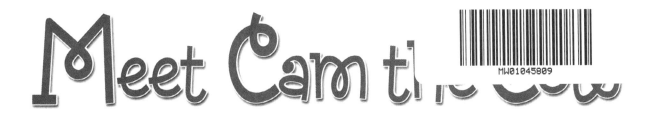

By Rosa Perez

Illustrated by Amy Loeffler

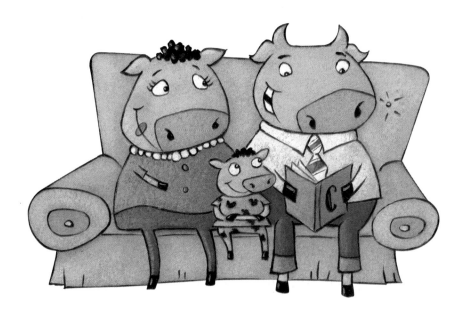

Target Skill Consonant Cc/k/

Scott Foresman
is an imprint of

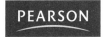

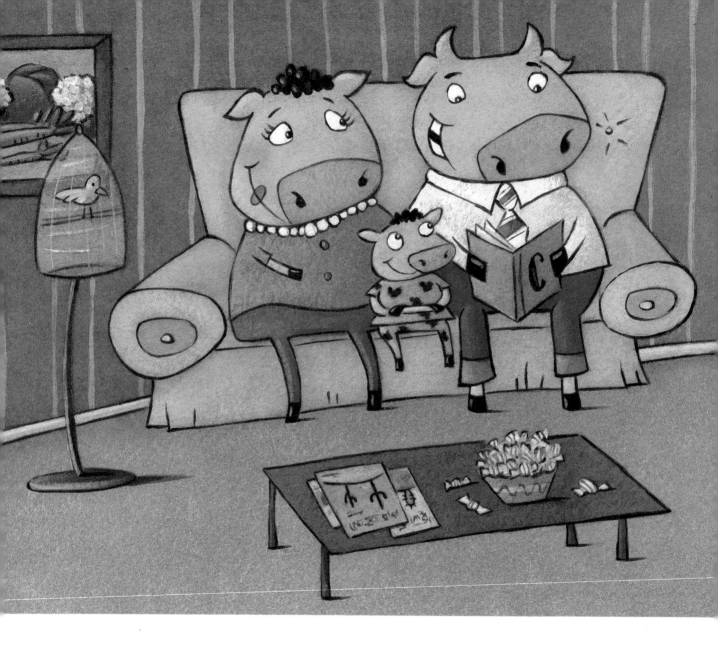

I am Cam.

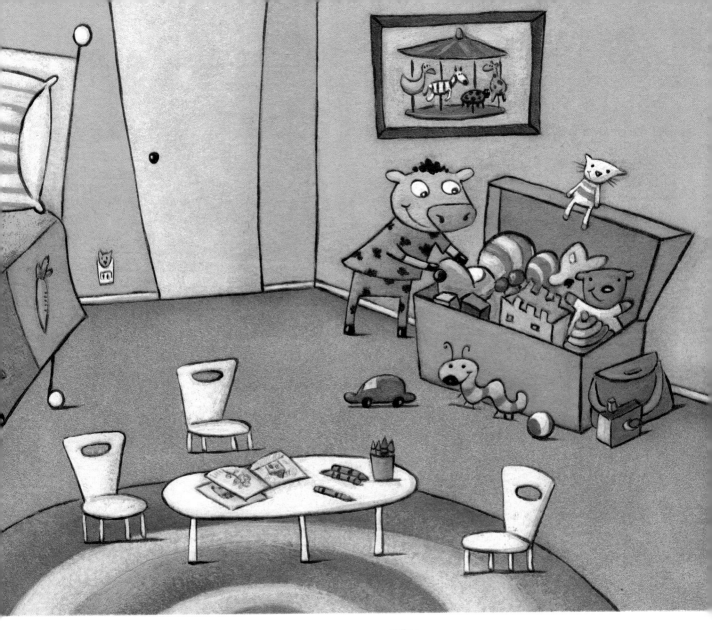

I am a cow.

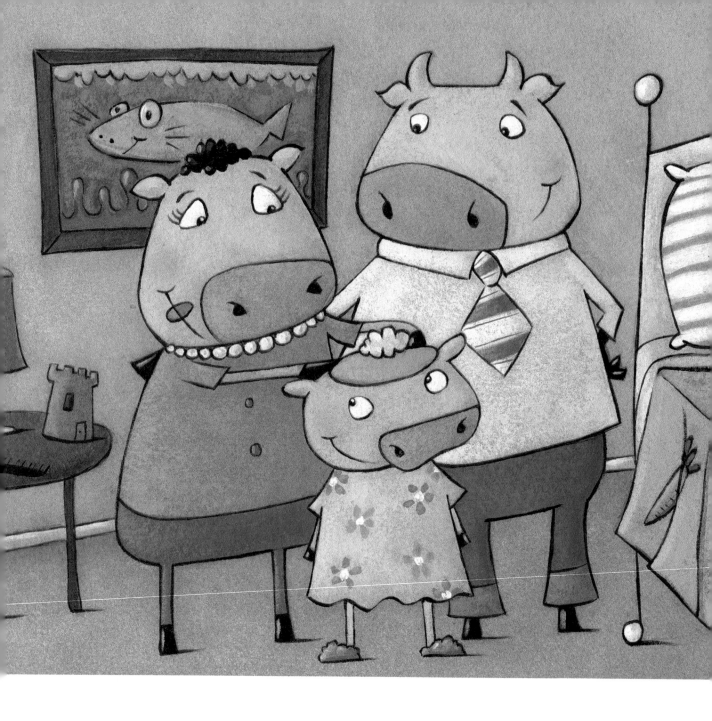

I have a little cap.

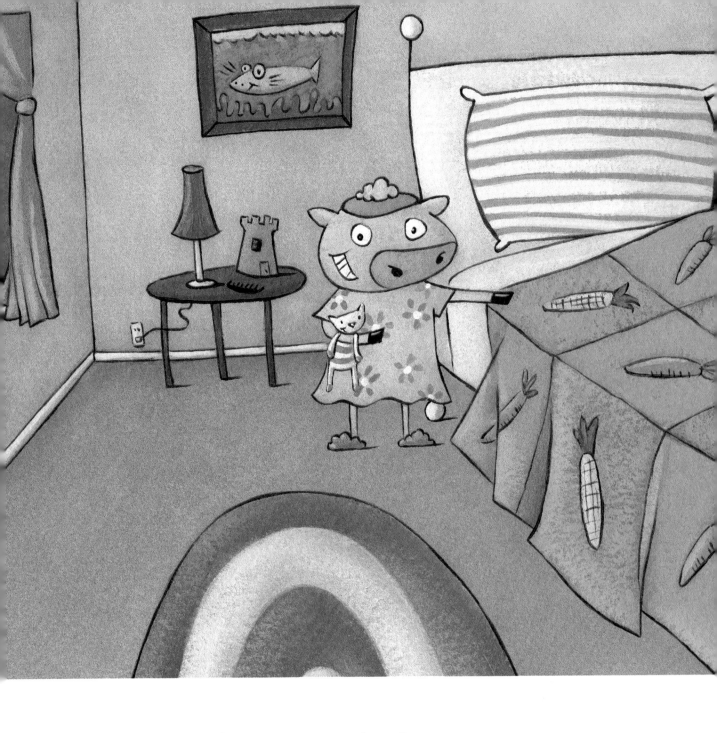

I have a little cat.

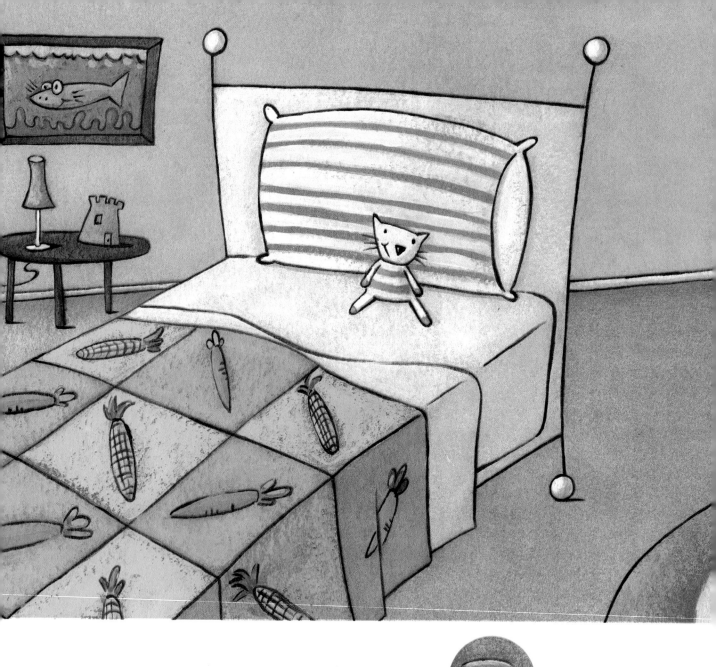

I have a little cup.

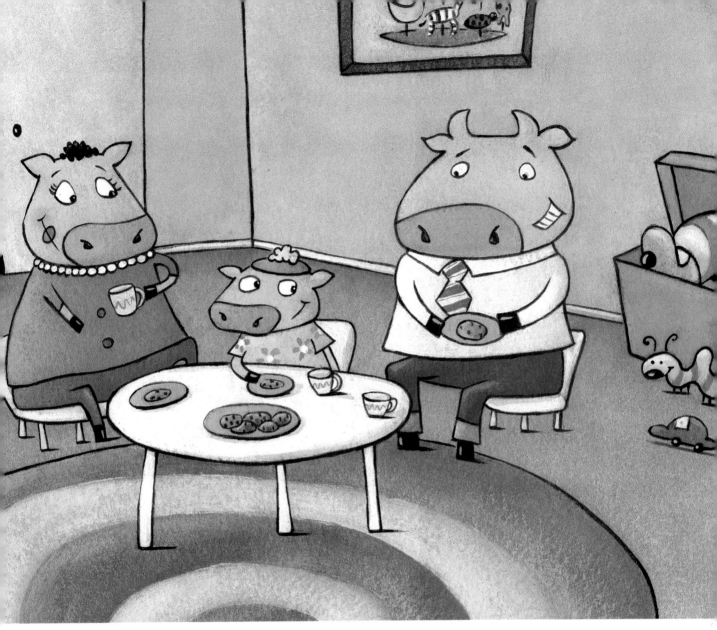

I have a little cookie.

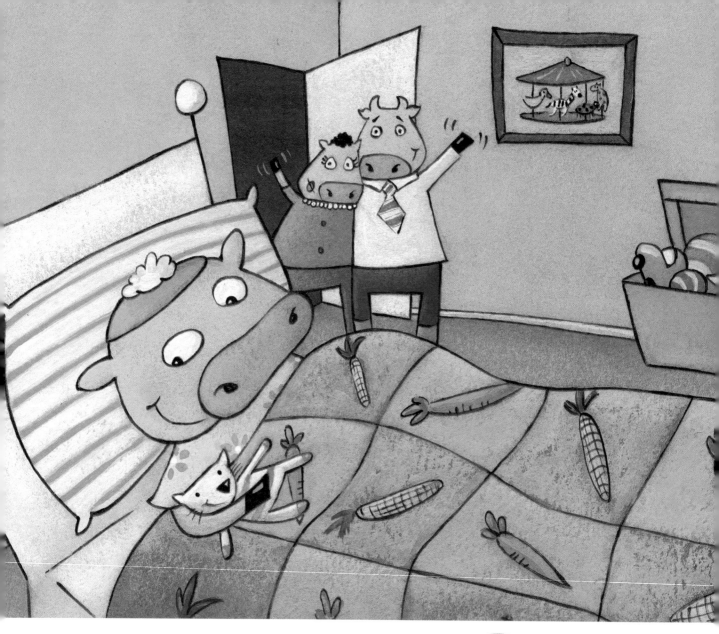

I have a little bed.